Be Not Afraid,
I Am with You

Be Not Afraid, I Am with You

Prayers for Healing

by
Mary Brian Durkin, OP

Saint Mary's Press
Christian Brothers Publications
Winona, Minnesota

Genuine recycled paper with 10% post-consumer waste. Printed with soy-based ink.

The publishing team included Carl Koch, development editor; Laurie A. Berg, copy editor; James H. Gurley, production editor; Hollace Storkel, typesetter; Maurine R. Twait, art director; Clare vanBrandwijk, illustrator; Tom Lowes, cover photo and design; pre-press, printing, and binding by the graphics division of Saint Mary's Press.

The acknowledgments continue on page 161.

Printed in the United States of America

Printing: 9 8 7 6 5 4 3 2 1

Year: 2007 06 05 04 03 02 01 00 99

ISBN 0-88489-583-1

Contents

Preface

As a hospital chaplain, I often hear patients complain despondently: "I just can't pray anymore. Not even the prayers I've said for years." In response I'm tempted to answer: "You are ill, in pain, worried, wondering what will happen next. No wonder you can't relax enough to pray."

But to anyone suffering spiritual dryness, that comment would bring little comfort. Instead, I quote Teresa of Ávila's advice: "The very fact that you desire to pray is in itself a prayer; and God knows that, so stop worrying about it." There are many ways to pray, even when we don't feel up to it or our prayers seem as dry as sawdust.

It is my hope that the prayers and suggestions for different ways to pray offered in this book will help you to dialog with your Divine Healer, for that is what prayer really is—a dialog, an intimate sharing of heartfelt thoughts.

Praying the Prayers in This Book

The prayers in this book offer words to use to talk with God, especially when you are at a loss for what to say, when pain seems overwhelming, when fear has you in its clutches.

Find the prayers that you need. Do not worry about starting from the beginning of the book and praying until the end. Pray the words that best suit your mood, your needs at the moment. Pray your favorites every hour, whenever you need them. Let the prayers become like good friends that you invite into your soul whenever you need their wisdom and consolation.

If you can, pray the words slowly and let them speak to you. Ponder any line or word that seems specially written to you. Repeat it. Savor it.

Jesus invites us "to pray always and not to lose heart" (Luke 18:1). Recall these words before you begin a prayer. Have confidence in his promise.

Some Thoughts About Other Ways to Pray

Even when you are ill, each day offers new ways to praise and worship your Friend. That lukewarm, unappetizing tray; the incessant blaring of your roommate's television; the interminably long wait for assistance; every painful procedure—all these tribulations can become treasures of grace.

A smile, a cheery greeting to the nurse—even though you know she is going to stick a needle in your arm, words of praise and gratitude for tasks well done—all are prayers because your words and actions tell those ministering to you that you recognize Jesus Christ, the divine healer, in them. May they, in turn, see Christ in you.

And don't forget to see God's compassionate love for you in joyful situations, too: the touch of a friendly hand, the card that makes you chortle aloud, the phone call that eases your anxiety or assures you of continued prayers for your recovery. Prayers of gratitude surely delight the Giver of all good gifts.

We need to be reminded of Thomas Merton's words in *The Living Bread:* "In modern times we have lost sight of the fact that even the most ordinary actions of our everyday life are invested, by their very nature, with a deep spiritual meaning."

Michael Downey, in *Clothed in Christ,* reinforces this: "Every activity, even the most mundane, is, at least potentially, sacramental activity." When we consider that bread and water are the ordinary materials of sacramental life, it helps us understand that every action of our mundane day can also be sacramental if offered to God as a prayer.

Think of every trial, every painful moment and tedious hour, as sacraments of the present moment that will further your healing by encouraging you to make good use of this time of illness. You may not have a nice, comfy feeling while doing this, but it is the will, not feelings, that counts. Offer to God every minute of those healing hours, your sacramental effort to further your own healing.

Praying Any Way You Can

So many times patients who have been sick
for a long period or who are in great pain
exclaim despondently: "I try to pray, but
before I know it, I'm distracted. The phone
rings, nurses come in to give medications,
and finally, when it is quiet again, I'm just
too frazzled to concentrate." Many factors
deter us from praying, even when we truly
desire to do so. May I offer some suggestions
to help you cope when it is difficult to pray?

First, stop thinking that you must pray
when you are in pain. Don't even attempt
to say your usual prayers. God knows your
condition—physical, mental, and spiritual—
and understands you even better than you
do yourself. God desires your love, not many
words.

Second, when you wish to pray, just quiet
down, relax. Try talking casually, informally
to God, just as you would chat with the
patient who shares your room or with a close
friend who pops in for a visit. Talk freely.
Express what you are feeling and experi-
encing at the moment. Yes, even if you are

angry and upset with God. Your Creator and Sustainer can take it.

Experiment with short one- or two-sentence prayers, such as a heartfelt plea: "Lord, help me now" or "Christ, you experienced many types of suffering; help me to bear this." Try a bit of cajolery: "I'm hurting, Jesus. Be my good Samaritan!" Try short prayers of gratitude: "Thanks, healing Christ, for the peaceful night!" or "I'm so grateful, Jesus Christ, for your support." After a little practice, these quick prayers will become an integral part of your everyday prayer life.

Praying Without Words

A simple way to pray without formal words is to select a specific name or title given to Jesus, such as Friend or Teacher, then think for a few minutes about when and how Christ has played that special role in your life. Use the familiar analogy of Christ as shepherd. When was he a kind shepherd to you? Perhaps when he wisely guided you to make the decision to consult a physician? Or when he led you along a new path to a different job? a relationship that opened up fresh possibilities? looked after you when you needed care? After pondering specific instances of Jesus' shepherding you, thank him for his care. It's that simple!

From the list below, select a name that appeals to you; then ponder how Christ has played that role in your life. You don't need words, just loving thoughts. Your reflections are prayers precious beyond words.

Shepherd	Teacher	Samaritan
Companion	Guide	Physician
Rock	Healer	Mentor
Friend	Rescuer	Brother

Praying with the Scriptures

Pondering the words of the Scriptures reveals the love of God, the compassion of Jesus, and the wisdom of the Holy Spirit. We strengthen our faith, our courage, and our trust in the providence of our God. Taking a few minutes each day to think about one or two of the following quotations can bring you an inner peace and an abiding trust, and can become a silent prayer of praise and gratitude. The more frequently you practice this type of prayer, the easier and more satisfying it will become for you. Read, reread, and ponder slowly one of the following passages or another favorite of your own.

May the spoken words of my mouth,
the thoughts of my heart,
win favor in your sight, O Yahweh,
my Redeemer, my Rock!

(Psalm 19:14)

Your people find refuge
in the shelter of your wings.

(Psalm 36:7)

They had come to hear [Jesus], and to be healed of their diseases; and those who were troubled with unclean spirits were cured. (Luke 6:18)

I sought Yahweh who answered me
and freed me from all my fears.

(Psalm 34:4)

How often have I desired to gather your children together as a hen gathers her brood under her wings. (Luke 13:34)

My sheep hear my voice. I know them, and they follow me. I give them eternal life, and they will never perish. No one will snatch them out of my hand. (John 10:27–28)

Let us therefore approach [God's] throne of grace with boldness, so that we may receive mercy and find grace to help in time of need. (Hebrews 4:16)

Let us not grow weary in doing what is right, for we will reap at harvest time, if we do not give up. (Galatians 6:9)

God did not give us a spirit of cowardice, but rather a spirit of power and of love and of self-discipline. (2 Timothy 1:7)

Stumbling Block or Stepping Stone? It's Your Choice!

While incarcerated in a Nazi prison camp, Victor Frankl wrote in his book *Man's Search for Meaning*, "Everything can be taken from us but one thing: the last of our freedoms— the freedom to choose one's attitude in any given set of circumstances, to choose one's own way."

Sometimes I hesitate to quote this profound truth, for fear that someone may interpret it as a directive to accept suffering just for the sake of suffering. "God sent this illness for a reason; he's punishing me so I'll be a better person" is not only a silly and dangerous attitude but also poor theology. The Creator God wants us to be whole and holy. Never doubt that.

Suffering in any form can destroy or purify, become a stumbling block or a stepping stone to wholeness. It is not the quantity of pain, its length, or its intensity that makes the difference, but the quality of our inner attitude, our heart's outlook. Theologians remind us that the term *heart* in the biblical sense means the whole person: heart and soul, mind and body.

Take some time to honestly evaluate your attitude toward your present situation. What have you chosen: apathy or optimism? cowardice or courage? anger or acceptance? torpidity or trust in God's healing providence? Only you can make the right choice. The greatest honor you can give to Almighty God is to live gladly, with fervent hope, because you realize that you are loved by God.

During times of sickness and suffering, it is not always easy to be a source of light and love to others, but take a little time each day to reflect on ways you can show that you truly appreciate the care and concern others show to you. Murmur a prayer of gratitude for each person, thank them warmly and graciously, and you will feel God's love enfolding both of you. What surer way to live in intimacy with the true Caregiver?

Morning Prayers

A Favorite Morning Offering

O God, creator of all,
   I offer you my prayers, works,
joys, and sufferings of this day.
I join myself with all your people
in praying for the salvation of souls,
the reunion of all Christians,
the grace of repentance,
the forgiveness of past sins,
and the wisdom to lead a holy life.
I wish to make my life this day
a loving prayer for [mention name
      or intention].
May every minute of my day
give you glory, honor, and praise.

Traditional Offering

*H*eavenly Father,
I offer you this day
all that I shall think or do or say,
uniting it with what was done
by Jesus Christ, your only Son.

A Morning Prayer

*D*ear God,
    creator of light,
I thank you for allowing me
to awaken to the light of a new day.
May the greatest of all lights, your love,
rise like the sun within my heart today.
Despite worries, pains, frustrations,
help me to radiate your peace to all
        whom I meet.
Then when the evening shadows come,
I can face the night, knowing that
by showing kindness, patience, and love
        to others,
I have glorified you and your Son,
        Jesus the Christ,
who is truly the light of the world. Amen.

A Prayer at Dawn

*L*isten to the exhortation of the Dawn!
Look to this day. . . .
For yesterday is but a dream,
and tomorrow is only a vision;
but today, well-lived, makes
every yesterday a dream of happiness,
and every tomorrow a vision of hope.
Look well therefore to this day!
Such is the salutation of the Dawn!

(An ancient Sanskrit poem)

A Prayer on Rising

*R*ule over me this day, O God,
 leading me on the path of righteousness.
Put your Word in my mind
and your Truth in my heart,
that this day I neither think nor feel anything
except what is good and honest.
Protect me from all lies and falsehood,
      helping me to discern
deception wherever I meet it.
Let my eyes always look straight ahead
on the road you wish me to tread,
that I might not be tempted
      by any distraction.
And make my eyes pure, that no false desires
may be awakened within me.

(Jacob Boehme)

Bless All Who Worship You

*B*less, O God,
all who worship you,
from the rising of the sun
until its going down.
Of your goodness, give us;
with your love, inspire us;
by your spirit, guide us;
by your power, protect us.
In your mercy,
bless us now
and always. Amen.

(An ancient collect)

Protect Me

*E*verlasting God,
you have brought me safely
to the beginning of a new day.
With your same loving care,
protect me from evil throughout this day.
Let no harm come to me, and keep me
from hurting others whom I encounter today,
ever remembering your words:
"Love one another as I have loved you."
Help me to show love, concern, and interest
to each person who ministers to me today.
Whether it be the one who brings me a tray,
the transport worker who wheels me
        to therapy or tests,
the nurse who takes my vital signs,
or the volunteer who delivers my mail,
they all contribute to my healing
        and recovery.
By my warm, personal response,
let me show my gratitude and love for them.

Searching for God

My God,
teach my heart this day where and
how to see you,
where and how to find you.

You have made me and remade me,
and you have bestowed on me
all the good things I possess,
and still I do not know you.
I have not yet done that
for which I was made.

Teach me to seek you,
for I cannot seek you
unless you teach me,
or find you
unless you show yourself to me.

Let me seek you in my desire,
Let me desire you in my seeking.
Let me find you by loving you,
Let me love you when I find you.

(Saint Anselm)

A Prayer of Acceptance

Gracious God,
please help me to live today
quietly, hopefully,
leaning on your sustaining strength.
Give me the grace to endure whatever comes
patiently, serenely;
to accept discomfort and pain
without undue complaint;
to greet caregivers, family, and friends
gratefully, joyfully;
and as for tomorrow,
ditto, ditto. Please!

Prayer for a Blessed Day

*H*oly Friend, you promised
   never to forsake those
who truly love you, and so with confidence
I ask you to bless this day and all that occurs.
When I am troubled, help me to remember
how patiently you endured unmerited pain
   for my sake.
When I am irritable, help me to recall
   your words:
"My peace I give to you. . . . Do not let
   your heart be troubled. . . . Do not
   be afraid. . . . I am with you always.
   . . . Ask and you shall receive."
Centuries ago when you walked this earth,
you showed love to so many people—
healing, forgiving, encouraging
all who sought your help.
Please heed my plea:
Lift up my heart; help me to forget my pain
   and troubles.
Show me how to be caring and responsive
   to others' needs
so that my love will be a reminder of you
   and your promises.

A Prayer for Courage and Patience

O God,
I beg you to give me the courage
and patience
needed throughout this day.
Help me to bear discomfort and indignities
without complaint,
sustain me in moments of discouragement,
calm me when I am overly anxious,
save me from grumbling and self-pity.

My God,
I desire this day to be one of spiritual growth,
a time to grow closer to you,
to remember your many kindnesses to me,
particularly when you sustained me
by giving me courage, strength, and healing.
You are the true physician;
please bless me and be with me all this day.

Making These Days Count

L oving God,
   I worship you.
I ask you in your compassion, please
strengthen my faith,
deepen my trust,
so that these days of healing and recuperation
will be days of grace.
As I am renewed in health of mind, body,
      and spirit,
may I grow closer to you,
who already has given me so many gifts:
the concerned care of wise physicians,
skillful nurses, supportive family and friends.
Most important of all these is
your sustaining, healing presence,
      day and night.
For all your past favors, I thank you,
and beg your blessing on these days
      of recuperation.
I know that every day will be a challenge.
May each one also be spiritually rewarding.

A Prayer for Strength to Be One's Best

*A*lmighty God,
please take from me all that prevents me
from being less than you desire me to be.
I realize that my physical pain,
my bitterness over past disappointments,
my fears for today
and anxiety about tomorrow,
all keep me from being the Christlike person
you would like me to be.
Help me to think more about the blessings
you have given me, and less about my pains
that are so slight compared to Christ's
    sufferings
endured patiently for my redemption.
May your love and compassion
strengthen me,
support me,
inspire me
to live up to my best potential:
to be what you desire me to be,
today and always.

For a Serene and Quiet Heart

O loving God,
please give me a serene and quiet heart.
If there is anxiety and stress today,
bless me with a bit of your tranquillity,
so that even when I'm troubled or in pain,
I may radiate peace of mind and heart,
and complete trust in your provident care.
As I try to emulate your serenity today,
perhaps someone who ministers to me
    or comes to visit me,
by some little act or words of mine,
may glimpse your goodness
    and sustaining peace.

I Offer You, Lord

I offer you, Lord, my thoughts: to be
fixed on you;
my words: to have you for their theme;
my actions: to reflect my love for you;
my sufferings: to be endured
        for your greater glory.
I want to do what you ask of me:
in the way you ask,
for as long as you ask,
because you ask it.
Lord, enlighten my understanding,
strengthen my will,
purify my heart,
and make me holy.
Let me love you, my Lord and my God,
and see myself as I really am:
a pilgrim in this world,
a Christian called to respect and love
all those whose lives I touch.

· · · · · · · · · · · · · ·

Help me to conquer anger with gentleness,
greed by generosity,
apathy by fervor.
Help me to forget myself
and reach toward others.

Make me prudent in planning,
courageous in taking risks.
Make me patient in suffering,
unassuming in prosperity.
Keep me, Lord, attentive at prayer,
temperate in food and drink,
diligent in my work,
firm in my good intentions.

(Pope Clement XI)

Lord, Come into My Heart

O Lord,
come into my heart,
and by your power
draw me to yourself.
Grant me today
charity and compassion.
Keep me, O Christ,
from every evil thought, word, and action.
Kindle within me a burning desire
to serve you faithfully.
Help me this day in every trouble,
O Christ. May your will be mine.

(Thomas Aquinas)

Send Down Your Spirit, O God

O God,
who has taught us that any deeds
accomplished without love are worthless,
send down your Holy Spirit,
and pour into our hearts
that most excellent gift of love,
the very bond of peace and virtue
without which whoever lives is counted dead
    before you.
Grant this for the sake of your only Son,
    Jesus Christ. Amen.

(*The Book of Common Prayer*)

The Love of God

*W*e have known and believe
the love that God has for us.
God is love,
and those who abide in love
abide in God,
and God abides in them.

(1 John 4:16)

Strengthen and Support Me Today

Savior Jesus Christ,
strengthen and support me
during this day.
Quiet my fears;
free me, please, from
aggravating anxieties,
barren brooding,
tormenting thoughts.
Grace me with sincere contrition,
compassion, and all-embracing charity,
so that throughout this day,
recalling at times your Passion and death,
I may more fully comprehend
your everlasting love for me.
Inspired by your selfless self-giving,
may I continue to strive to be
all that you desire me to be:
a loving witness to your generous love.

Trusting in Your Word, O God

*T*rusting in your word, O God,
  we wait for your Spirit.
Send him forth from the holy heavens
to sanctify our hearts,
which, without him, are empty
      and without focus.
Perhaps in those depths of our being
there are secrets hidden;
desires and tendencies we dare not
      acknowledge
even to ourselves.
Enter these hidden places—
burn, purify, transform.
We are not able by ourselves
      to help ourselves.
We wait upon you and your Holy Spirit.
                    (Evelyn Underhill)

Lord, I Seek You

*L*ord, I seek you with all my heart,
   with all the strength you have given me.
I long to understand that which I believe.
You are my only hope;
please listen to me.
Do not let my weariness lessen my desire
to find you, to see your face.
You created me in order to find you;
you gave me strength to seek you.
My strength and my weakness
     are in your hands:
preserve my strength, and help my weakness.
Where you have already opened the door,
let me come in; where it is shut,
open at my knocking.
Let me always remember you, love you,
meditate upon you, and pray to you
until you restore me to your perfect pattern.
(Augustine)

O Father

O Father,
  light up the small duties of this day's life:
may they shine with the beauty
    of [your] countenance.
May we believe that glory may dwell
in the commonest task of every day.

(Augustine)

Father, Strengthen Me

*F*ather,
strengthen me by your Holy Spirit
to carry out my mission
of changing the world
or some definite part of it
for the better.
Make me more energetic
in setting to rights
what I see wrong in the world
instead of just complaining about it.
Never let me forget
that it is far better
to light one candle
than to curse the darkness. Amen.

(A Christopher prayer)

Teach Us, Good Lord

*T*each us, good Lord,
to serve you as you deserve;
to give and not count the cost;
to fight and not heed the wounds;
to toil and not seek for rest;
to labor and not ask for reward
save that of knowing we do your will
through Jesus Christ our Lord.

(Ignatius Loyola)

A Prayer for God's Gifts Today

Gracious, loving, and generous God,
you are the giver of all good gifts,
and so I dare to ask you to help me.
When I am troubled and upset,
     give me your serenity.
When I am depressed and disconsolate,
     comfort me.
When I am tormented by regrets and failures,
     solace me.
When I am lonely, unloved, unwanted,
     walk with me.
When I am distressed by my illness and pain,
touch me with your healing, everlasting love,
so that I may become more like you:
responsive to the needs of others,
showing them compassion and love,
forbearance and selfless generosity.
Help me to make this time in my life
a way to show that I want to follow your ways
and to give others the gifts
     you have given to me.

A Prayer of Dedication

*T*ake and receive, O Lord,
   all my liberty, my memory,
my understanding, all my will.
All that I have and possess,
you have given to me.
I restore it all to you.
I surrender it in order that
you may dispose of it
according to your will.
Only give me your love and your grace
and I shall be rich enough,
and shall seek nothing more.

(Ignatius Loyola)

A Prayer for Obedience to God's Plans

*L*ord,
grant that I may always allow myself
to be guided by you,
always follow your plans,
and perfectly accomplish your holy will.
Grant that in all things,
great and small,
today and all the days of my life,
I may do whatever you may require of me.
Help me to respond to the slightest
prompting
of your grace, so that I may be your
trustworthy instrument
for your honor.
May your will be done in time and eternity—
by me, in me, and through me. Amen.

(Teresa of Ávila)

A Reminder: God Has a Plan

God has created me
to do some definite service.
God has committed some work to me
  which has not been committed to another.
I have my mission—
I am a link in a chain,
  a bond of connection between persons.
God has not created me without reason.
I shall do good; I shall do God's work.
Therefore, I will trust God.
Whatever, wherever I am,
I am always useful.
When I am in sickness, my sickness
        may serve God;
if I am in sorrow, my sorrow may serve God.
God does nothing in vain.
God knows what is in mind for me.
I trust my God, my creator, my redeemer.
                    (John Henry Cardinal Newman)

A Prayer of Trust in God's Providence

*M*y Lord God,
    I have no idea where I am going.
I do not see the road ahead of me;
I cannot know for certain where it will end.
Nor do I really know myself,
and the fact that I think I am following
your will does not mean that
    I am actually doing so.
But I believe that the desire to please you
does in fact please you.
And I hope that I have that desire in all that
    I am doing.
I hope that I will never do anything
apart from that desire.
And I know that if I do this
you will lead me by the right road,
though I may know nothing about it.
Therefore will I trust you always
though I may seem to be lost
    and in the shadow of death.
I will not fear, for you are ever with me,
and you will never leave me
    to face my perils alone.

(Thomas Merton)

Nothing Is Merely an Accident

I have an ever deeper and firmer belief
that nothing is merely an accident
when seen in the light of God—
that my whole life,
        down to the smallest details,
has been marked out for me
in the plan of Divine Providence
and has a completely coherent meaning
in God's all-seeing eyes.

(Edith Stein)

Wilderness

*N*o Christian," states Evelyn Underhill,
"escapes a taste of the wilderness
on the way to the promised land."

Dear God,
put into our hearts a firm desire
to get involved in your plan
for a better world.
Regardless of the pain it may cost,
strengthen us to work for peace and justice,
today and every day.
Help us to recall what others
have suffered in order to
        bring about your Reign.

Mary Stuart's Prayer

Keep me, O God, from all pettiness;
  let me be large
in thought, in word, in deed.
Let me be done with fault-finding
and leave off all self-seeking.
May I put away all pretense
and meet others face to face
without self-pity and without prejudice.
May I never be hasty in judgment
and always generous.
Let me take time for all things, and
make me grow calm, serene, and gentle.
Teach me to put into action
my better impulses,
straightforward and unafraid.
Grant that I may realize that
it is the little things of life
that create differences,
that in the big things of life
we are one.
And, O Lord God,
let me not forget to be kind.

A Caregiver's Morning Prayer

*D*ear God,
    as I start out today to minister to
    others in your name,
give me, please, your very special gifts
    and grace:
your insight to perceive the needs of the ill,
your wisdom to respond holistically,
your grace to listen with compassion,
your courage to endure, despite rebuffs
    and risks,
your insight into ways to help others
    help themselves.
Above all, Lord,
let me be kind and caring, as you were.
"I can do all things
through him who strengthens me."
(Philippians 4:13)

May Your Will Be Mine

O Lord,
may your will be mine.
Help me to seek for it,
to find it, to accomplish it,
as you desire.
Show me your ways,
teach me your virtues,
enable me to follow your laws
today and to the end of my life.

Help me, O Lord,
to grow in love of you.
Grant that our inner conversations
        may never cease.
Enlighten me to see all
that you wish me to accomplish.
Let me never stand in the way of the grace
which, through me, should be poured out
upon those whom I meet.

(Thomas Aquinas)

In Praise of the Divine Overseer

*I*n the name of God, Divine Giver,
praise be your name forever,
the God who always was,
always is, and always will be,
from whom alone is the law derived.
With all my strength, I offer you
gratitude, praise, obedience.
May all my words,
deeds, desires, and thoughts
keep your laws.
May I always keep pure
the six powers:
thought, speech, work,
memory, mind, and understanding.
May I accomplish this day and always
your plans for me according to your will.
Praise be to you,
the Overseer,
the Lord,
most Worthy of all Worthy.

(An early Persian prayer)

Loving Father, Teach Me

*L*oving Father,
perfect teacher, patient guide
in these troubled times;
sitting with you,
the perfect One,
I take the influence of your company
to teach me the way of reconciliation,
wisdom and harmony.
I see you,
the embodiment of all solutions
for the world and myself at this time.
Touch my heart
and my conscience daily,
that all I do
will work toward
your goal of perfection
and peace for all.

(An anonymous Hindu prayer)

The Psalmist Speaks

You who dwell in the shelter of the Most
  High,
who abide in the shadow of the Almighty,
say: "My Refuge and my Strength,
my God in whom I trust."
For God will save you from the snare
    of the fowler,
from the destroying pestilence.
With pinions God will cover you,
and under God's wings you shall find refuge;
God's faithfulness is a guard and a shield.
You will not fear the terror of the night
nor the arrow that flies by day.

. . . .

God declares:
"Because you cling to me, I will deliver you;
I will protect you because you acknowledge
    my name.
You shall call upon me and I will answer you.
I will be with you in times of trouble;
I will deliver you and glorify you
and will show you my salvation."

(Psalm 91:1–5,14–16)

Prayers
for Special Times

Prayer to Christ, the Divine Healer

So many times in the past, Divine Healer,
you have consoled me, and so once again
   I come
to beg your intercession and aid.
I ask you to dispel or alleviate
the anxieties that trouble me,
the fears that torment me,
this illness that weakens me,
and all the frustrations, pain, and suffering
that these constantly bring.
Divine Healer, help me to feel
your caring presence in my misery,
your compassion in my difficulties,
your forgiveness in my failure
   to be accepting,
and most of all, please
continue to sustain me with your
   understanding love.
Please hold me, uplift me with your
   healing grace.

Prayer for Emotional Stability

God, my sustainer,
help all of us who need emotional
    stability.
Please give us patience, hope, and strength
to cope with all our problems,
and to seek and accept assistance.
May you give us the grace and wisdom
to accept ourselves as we are now,
to place ourselves under your protection,
to follow wisely those who minister
        in your name,
to believe that you will guide them
        to help us.
May you continue to inspire our trust
        in your promise:
"Behold, I stand at the door and knock.
If anyone hears my voice and opens the door,
I will come in."
Sustainer, help us to open the door
        of our hearts,
to welcome you, the most caring of guests,
and to cooperate with those helping us
        in your name.

To accomplish our goal, emotional stability,
we need your healing grace in our lives.
Come. Enter. Welcome. Remain with us.
    Please!

Prayer Before Undergoing a Worrisome Procedure

Divine Companion,
placing myself in your compassionate
care,
I beg you to be with me during these
next hours.
Please deepen my trust in you, so that
I will not be fearful or worried
as I undergo this difficult procedure.
Calm my heart and mind, relax my body,
and grant me
the assurance expressed in Psalm 4:
"As soon as I lie down, I peacefully go
to sleep;
you alone, my Strength, keep me
perfectly safe" (v. 8).

Prayer Before Surgery

*C*reator of us all,
    you know every fiber of my being.
Graciously give your knowledge
        to my surgeon
and to all who assist in this operation.
Enlighten their minds, guide their hands,
steady their nerves, bless each procedure.
As I am wheeled under the bright lights,
may my fears be replaced by a sense
        of your presence
as I murmur, "Loving God, I place my trust
        in you."
Bless my family and friends
        nervously awaiting the outcome;
give them peace of mind and confidence
        in your providential care.
After the surgery is completed,
may thoughts of your Son, Jesus,
strengthen me to bear my pain without
        self-pity or complaints.
Loving God,
I beg you to answer my requests,
not in proportion to my merits but
in the bounty of your caring compassion.
        Amen.

(Heal Me, Lord)

Prayer Before an Operation

O merciful God,
I turn in prayerful confidence to you,
who healed the sick and comforted the weak.
I put all my trust in you, and although
I must admit that I am a bit anxious now,
yet I know that you will be with me
these next hours.
Please, bless me with courage and patience,
and give wisdom, skill, and healing power
to my physician and to all who assist
in this procedure.
Be with me now and during the days
of recuperation,
so that I may have the fortitude
to endure pain
without too many complaints.
Gracious God, I trust you completely
to get me through this ordeal.
Thank you!

Prayer After Surgery

Source of all healing, please accept
my heartfelt gratitude
    for bringing me safely
through this operation and supporting me
during the first long hours in recovery.
Forgive my fears and complaints;
please continue to heal and comfort me.
Ease my discomfort,
calm my anxieties,
bless me with your patience.
I am deeply grateful to you and to all
who are ministering to my needs
        in your name.
When I have regained my strength
        and health again,
I promise to acknowledge your goodness
        to me
by leading a life that truly glorifies you,
        my God; your Son, Jesus the Christ;
        and the Holy Spirit.

Prayer After an Operation

God, my God,
I can't thank you sufficiently
for bringing me through
this operation so successfully
and for preserving my life.
Continue, please, to rest your healing hands
on me,
and on my physician, my nurses, and other
staff members
who are helping me on the road to recovery.
I know there will be pain, discomfort,
and anxiety.
May I keep on asking for your assistance?
Help me remember during the difficult times
ahead
your hours of pain on your journey
to Calvary.
Just as your torments were endured
to redeem us,
may my sufferings, offered in love,
bear fruit in wisdom, compassion,
and courage
for myself as well as for my family, friends,
and caregivers,
who have prayed for and assisted in
my recovery.

Thank you, Source of all consolation,
for your healing strength.
Continue to sustain me so that, restored
        to health,
I can serve you faithfully.

Prayer of Gratitude

*T*hanks be to you, our savior Jesus Christ!
In all my pain, anxieties, and illness,
you have given me the gift of fortitude
to bear it all with some dignity and grace,
always trusting in your healing love.
I hope that during these days of pain
and healing
I have realized again the depth of your
compassionate care.
About this I am certain:
I will lead a better life from now on,
for this illness has made me
focus on what is truly important:
to follow your way of love, justice, and peace.

Prayer to Discern God's Will

*L*iving and true God,
grant that by the guidance
of the Holy Spirit,
we may discern your holy will
in this situation;
and by the grace of the same Spirit,
we may be strengthened to accomplish it
with peace of mind and heart,
despite the sorrow and pain the decision
may cost us.
This we ask of you in the name of your Son,
Jesus Christ.

While Waiting for a Transplant

Compassionate Creator,
although I realize my condition is
serious,
I find myself rather amused when I read
some of the verses in Psalm 139:
"It was you who formed me. . . .
I am wonderfully made."
Well, that may be true,
but right now I am lacking a vital part!
As you well know, I have been hoping
and praying
that there will be an organ donor soon.
I have mixed feelings when I pray about
this need:
I don't wish anyone to die so that I may
continue to live.
Yet, I can't help wishing that more folks
understood
what a gift they can give to others
in serious need.
Now that I desperately need this transplant,
I realize that to give a part of yourself
so that another's life may be saved
is a priceless gift.

If I am ever blessed by such a gift,
I'll never stop praying for my benefactor
and thanking you, Almighty God,
creator and giver of all good gifts.

Prayer About
Removing Life-Support Systems

Come, Spirit of love, wisdom, and
    compassion,
be with all our family now
as we come together to discuss the physician's
        advice
that it is time to consider removing
the life-support system that for these
        past days
has artificially sustained the life of _____,
        our dear one.
Help us, loving God,
to express our thoughts honestly
while respecting the views of each person
        present.
Guide and direct us, so that after making
this momentous and difficult decision,
we will have peace in our hearts
        and with one another.
As we ponder and deliberate, help us
        to understand
that true life is eternal, that love
        is everlasting,
and that at death we do not really lose . . .
but only help to set free a cherished soul

from suffering and diminishment,
     longing for eternal peace.
Before we begin to discuss
     this awesome question
concerning the continuation or withdrawal
     of life supports,
let us join hands together
and say aloud the prayer that Jesus taught us:
"Our Father, . . ."

Prayer when Life Supports
Are to Be Removed

God of all creation,
   you know our sadness as we gather
      around the bedside
of _____, our dear one, who exists only
      by artificial means.
It's been heartbreaking to make this decision,
but we realize that it is selfish to prolong
      this stage.
Jesus, compassionate consoler,
as we say our final good-byes,
put your arms around _____ and around
      us, too,
for we need your support and comfort now
      more than ever.
Bless with your presence these last precious
      moments,
as we say farewell to one whom we have
      dearly loved.
Draw us closer to you, dear God,
so that we will always remain close
to the one we now help to release from pain
      and suffering.
Strengthened by our belief that life is eternal
and true love is everlasting, we ask you, God:

Come with your angels and saints
and welcome into resurrected life
one whom we love, and who, when able,
        served you so well.
Give eternal rest to our dear one,
and the joy that surpasses all understanding.
We ask this in Jesus' name.

Prayer of a Disabled Person

*L*oving God,
help me to accept without bitterness
   this disability
that suddenly has so altered my life.
Empower me to see beyond the limitations
   it imposes.
Teach me how to transform it into a blessing,
a means of deepening my trust and reliance
   on you.
Forgive my times of frustration, anger,
   and despondency.
I thank you for the lessons I am slowly
   learning:
the need to treat everyone with dignity,
particularly those who have any disability:
stroke victims, blind folks, those who are
   mentally impaired,
the fragile weak, and those who are
   paralyzed.
Loving God, I need to focus my energies
so that I can achieve whatever independence
   is possible.

I offer to you all the hours of my therapy
    sessions
as a silent prayer for all those worn out
    with pain,
for all children, especially those who are
    neglected and abused,
and for all the dying. Grant them peace
    at the last.
For myself, I beg for the gifts of patience
    and courage.
Continue, loving God, to bring healing to all
    in need.

(Heal Me, Lord)

Death of Her Baby:
A Mother's Anguished Prayer

God, I'm confused and angry.
　　Never before have I talked to you
with such bitterness in my heart,
but now, upset, resentful, crushed, I cry out:
"Why did I lose my baby? Why my child?"
Every day of this pregnancy, I've followed
　　　the rules:
exercise, diet, checkups—everything!
　　　Prayers, too.
And yet my baby died. Why did you fail
　　　to help?
Do you know the anguish, the emptiness
　　　I feel?
My disappointment after waiting
　　　all these months?
I'm upset, distraught, weak, and in pain,
yet I know I must calm down and take care
of things that must be done; so much
　　　has changed now.
Why did it happen?
God, forgive my anger.
I know you did not cause this heartbreak.
I try not to blame you, for you are the giver
　　　of life,
not its destroyer.

But I am devastated, angry, and in turmoil.
Journey with me during these next
    difficult days.
I feel so empty, so bereft that only you
    can fill this void.
Surround me with your love,
    give me your peace,
and help me somehow to understand
    such suffering.

Prayer for a Sick Child

*J*esus, you showed your love for children
  many times and in many ways.
One day your disciples, noticing that you
      were weary,
tried to prevent some little children from
      running up
to talk to you, but you said kindly,
"Let those children come over here to me."
Then, gathering them around you, you
      blessed them
and prayed that they would always be safe
      from harm.
Knowing your love and concern
      for youngsters,
we are confident that you will hear
      and answer our plea
that our beloved child be restored to health.
Guide, please, the physicians, nurses,
      and all the staff
who are taking care of _____.
To all caretakers, give your healing touch,
your compassionate tenderness,
      your wisdom;

and bless all in our anxious family circle
with an ever-deepening trust in your love
   and concern.
All this we ask you, Divine Healer.

Prayer to Overcome an Addiction

*D*ear God, help me to face the truth
about my addiction.

I've been off balance for so long; now I want
to get my life in order again. Help me!
Help me to accept help.

I've taken the first step by ripping off the
masks that I've been hiding behind: the
bluff that everything was the fault of
others, my folks, my friends, my job,
lost dreams—everything was to blame,
except me. Not true! I am to blame;
help me, God, to face that truth.

The most difficult part is that when I admit
that I've failed myself and those I love,
I get so dejected that I lose the courage
to start over again.

A chaplain warned me:

"You won't help yourself by groveling in
guilt. God loves you now, but don't
forget that God loved you when you
were ruining your life, too. You see,
our God loves us even when we are
sinners—so shove the guilt. Start over,
but don't try to do it alone. Get help.
Now!"

The idea that you love me, despite my past, has given me some self-respect and courage. Strengthen me to accept help and healing, and if I start giving at up any time during the rehab program, please stretch out your hand to rescue me as you did Peter when he was sinking under the waves. I rely on your saving help now and in the days ahead. Hear my plea, dear Rescuer.

(Heal Me, Lord)

Prayer for Those with AIDS

*B*lessed are you, Lord of all,
giving new life and health to those who
call on you.
Gather into your Kingdom and manifest
your power
to heal all those with AIDS.
Blessed are you, Lord of wisdom,
who pushes back the borders of darkness
and disease.
Enlighten those who search for a cure
for AIDS,
and strengthen those who care
for our suffering brothers and sisters.
Blessed are you, Lord of love and peace;
be with the families and loved ones of those
who live with this disease.
Touch us all with your love
and make us instruments of your healing.
Blessed are you, Lord, in this sacrament
of body and blood.
Let us receive with joyful thanks
this true and living bread from heaven,
your reconciling light and life
throughout the ages.

(Found in Saint James Church,
Piccadilly, London)

Parents' Prayer for Their New Child

*D*ivine Giver of all good gifts,
how can we ever adequately thank you
for this child whom we have waited
    and yearned for?
As we look at this miracle of newness,
we are filled with relief and joy, but also
with awe when we think
    of the responsibilities
that face us in the years ahead.
You, God, were support and comfort
during those long months of waiting,
    and now
we turn to you again in thanksgiving
    and entreaty.
We beg you to continue to bless
    and sustain us.
Help us to be good parents as we nurture
    our child
along the way of happiness and holiness.
O God, guide us to mentor wisely,
    to discipline with wisdom
and love, following the example
    you have given us.

Bless our child, now and always,
        with the grace
needed to enjoy a life that will glorify you,
Jesus the Christ, and the Holy Spirit.

Prayer During Recuperation at Home

*H*oly Friend, I never realized how true
the old saying is:
"There's no place like home."
    For days I've looked
forward to returning home to family,
    my own bed,
home-cooked meals, visits from neighbors.
    But now
I'm worried! Things went smoothly
    at the hospital,
but what if something should go wrong
    at home?
Will help come quickly enough? Forgive me
for being anxious and thinking about myself
    so much.
I do trust you! Please help me to be patient
and cooperative with all those who are caring
    for me.
I don't want to be a burden or a worry
    to them.
I wish I could be like the Apostle Peter's
    mother-in-law:
after you healed her, she jumped up,
    able and strong,
ready to serve the whole household
    and guests!

Well, I know that my healing will take time.
Please walk with me each hour as I grow
    in strength;
help me to express my gratitude to all
    assisting me,
and thank you, Skillful Healer,
    for bringing me this far.

Prayer Before Holy Communion

*B*lessed Jesus,
I know very well that I am not worthy
    to receive you,
but despite that knowledge, I am so happy
    and comforted
by your willingness to come to me,
accepting me just as I am: weak, anxious,
    and suffering.
I need your gifts of strength
    and supportive love
to help me through these next few days.
My complete trust in your providence
    is as deep
as my love for you, which has grown
    immeasurably
during this time of sickness and stress.
Perhaps that is because I so often think
    of you—
healing the ill, comforting the troubled,
    so willingly
bearing trials, suffering, and a painful death.
I have so much to learn from your life
    on earth.
Come to me with your healing grace,
    dear welcome Guest!
Come and stay with me.

Prayer Before Taking Communion

O God of truth,
  help us to worthily receive
    this communion;
give us chastity in our bodies,
prudence and knowledge in our minds;
give us wisdom, God of mercies,
with our share of your holy body and blood.
                    (An early Christian prayer)

God, fill me with your love
so that I can be a Christ-bearer,
bringing you to others.

Prayer After Receiving Communion

Christ Jesus, I cannot thank you enough
for coming to me in this time of sickness.
Your presence strengthens, comforts,
   and sustains me
during all the trials, pain, and discomforts
   of each day.
Your love and healing power encourage me
and fill me with hope and trust
   as I ask you again
to restore me to health so that
   I can return home,
where I will serve you most faithfully.
For this precious gift of receiving you,
unworthy as I know I am, what can I say
except a heartfelt prayer of gratitude:
"Thank you. Thank you!"

Gracious God, Hear Our Prayer

O Jesus Christ,
comforter of the sad,
strength of the weak,
healer of the wounded,
consolation of the bereaved,
hear the prayers of the sick and the disabled,
the despondent, the careworn, the fragile,
who cry out to you for healing.
Journey with them as you did
    with your disciples
going to Emmaus; teach us that suffering
borne in your name is never lost.

Prayer for Letting Go

We seem to give them to you, O God,
who gave them first to us. Yet,
just as you did not
lose them in giving, so we do not really
lose them
when they return to you. For you give
not as the world gives, O Lord. What you
give,
you do not take away, and what is yours
is also ours,
if we belong to you.
Help us to realize that this life is eternal
and love is immortal; that death is only
a horizon,
and a horizon is nothing more than the limit
of sight.
Lift us up, O strong Son of God, that we may
see further;
cleanse our eyes that we may see more clearly;
draw us closer to you so that we may
know ourselves,
and be nearer to our beloved ones who are
now with you.

And while you prepare a place for us,
prepare us also for that happy place,
that where you are, we may also be
    forevermore.

                (Bede Jarrett)

Prayer for the Sick and the Dying

*L*ord Jesus Christ,
who in your last agony did commend
    your spirit
into the hands of your heavenly Father,
have mercy on the sick and the dying.
May death be for them the gate
    of everlasting life.
In their last hours of this life, fortify them
with the assurance of your presence even in
    the dark valley.
All this we ask in your name,
for you are the Resurrection and the Life,
to whom glory and praise are due,
forever and ever.

(The Sarum Primer)

Prayer for a Happy Death

O Lord and Saviour,
    help me in my last hour with your
        sacraments
and the sweetness of your grace.
Let your words of absolution be said over me,
and let your holy oils sign and seal me,
and let your holy body and blood be my food.
Let your holy Mother Mary come to me,
and my guardian angel whisper peace to me,
and your glorious saints and my patrons
        bless me,
that in them and through them all,
I may die as I desire to live,
in your church, in your faith,
and in your love. Amen.

(John Henry Cardinal Newman)

A Final Prayer

O Lord,
support us all the day long
of this troublesome life,
until the shadows lengthen
and the evening comes,
and the busy world is hushed,
and the fever of life is over,
and our work is done.
Then, Lord, in your great mercy,
grant us a safe lodging,
a holy rest,
and peace at the last,
though Jesus Christ, our Lord.

(John Henry Cardinal Newman)

Favorite Prayers
of Consolation

The Lord's Prayer

Our Father, who art in heaven,
hallowed be your name,
your kingdom come,
your will be done
on earth as it is in heaven.
Give us this day our daily bread, and
forgive us our trespasses
as we forgive those who trespass against us,
and lead us not into temptation
but deliver us from evil.
For the kingdom, the power, and the glory
are yours, now and forever.

De Profundis

Out of the depths I cry to you, O Lord!
Lord, hear my voice!
Let your ears be attentive
to the voice of my supplications.
If you, O Lord, mark my iniquities,
who shall endure it?
But with the Lord is forgiveness,
that you may be feared.
I wait for the Lord, my soul waits,
and in his word I hope;
my soul waits for the Lord
more than the watchmen await the dawn,
more than the watchmen wait for
      the morning!
O Israel, hope in the Lord,
for with the Lord there is steadfast love
and with him is plenteous redemption.
And he will redeem Israel
from all its iniquities.

Psalm 23

Yahweh, you are my shepherd;
  I shall not want.
In verdant pastures you give me repose.
Beside restful waters you lead me;
you refresh my soul.
You guide me in right paths
for your name's sake.
Even though I walk in the dark valley
I fear no evil;
for you are at my side.
Your rod and your staff give me courage.
You spread the table before me
in the sight of my foes.
You anoint my head with oil;
my cup brims over.
Only goodness and kindness follow me
all the days of my life;
and I shall dwell in your house
for years to come.

The Apostles' Creed

I believe in God, the Father Almighty,
  creator of heaven and earth;
and in Jesus Christ, his only Son, our Lord,
who was conceived by the Holy Spirit,
born of the virgin Mary,
suffered under Pontius Pilate,
was crucified, died, and was buried.
He descended into hell;
the third day he arose again from the dead.
He ascended into heaven
and sits at the right hand of God,
the Father Almighty;
from thence he shall come
to judge the living and the dead.
I believe in the Holy Spirit,
the holy catholic church,
the communion of saints,
the forgiveness of sins,
the resurrection of the body,
and life everlasting. Amen.

The Memorare

*R*emember, O most gracious virgin Mary,
that never was it known
that anyone who fled to your protection,
implored your help,
or sought your intercession
was left unaided.
Inspired by this confidence,
I come to you,
O virgin of virgins, my mother.
To you I come,
before you I stand,
sinful and sorrowful.
O mother of the Word Incarnate,
do not ignore my petitions,
but in your mercy,
hear and answer me. Amen.

Hail, Holy Queen

Hail, Holy Queen, Mother of Mercy,
  our life, our sweetness, and our hope!
To you we cry, poor banished children of Eve;
to you we send up our sighs,
mourning and weeping in this valley of tears.
Turn then, O most gracious advocate,
your eyes of mercy toward us,
and after this our exile,
show unto us the blessed fruit of your womb,
    Jesus.
O clement, O loving, O sweet Virgin Mary.
Pray for us, O holy Mother of God,
that we may be made worthy of the promises
    of Christ.

The Hail Mary

*H*ail, Mary, full of grace,
the Lord is with you.
Blessed are you among women,
and blessed is the fruit of your womb, Jesus.
Holy Mary, Mother of God,
pray for us sinners,
now and at the hour of our death. Amen.

Prayer of Saint Francis

*L*ord, make me an instrument of your
peace.
Where there is hatred, let me sow love;
where there is injury, pardon;
where there is doubt, faith;
where there is darkness, light;
and where there is sadness, joy.
O divine Master, grant that I may
not so much seek to be consoled
        as to console;
to be understood as to understand;
to be loved as to love.
For it is in giving that we receive;
it is in pardoning that we are pardoned;
and it is in dying that we are born
        to eternal life.

A Japanese Version of Psalm 23

*T*he Lord is my pace setter,
  I shall not rush.
He makes me stop for quiet intervals.
He provides me with images of stillness
which restore my serenity.
He leads me in the way of efficiency
through calmness of mind,
and his guidance is peace.
Even though I have a great many things
       to accomplish
each day, I will not fret, for his presence
       is here.
His timelessness, his all importance
will keep me in balance.
He prepares refreshment and renewal
in the midst of my activity by anointing
       my mind
with his oils of tranquillity.
My cup of joyous energy overflows.
Truly harmony and effectiveness shall be
the fruits of my hours for I shall walk
in the pace of my Lord
and dwell in his house forever.

(Life in the Spirit)

Come, Holy Spirit

Come, Holy Spirit,
  fill the hearts of your people.
Kindle in us the fire of your love.
Send forth your spirit,
and we shall be created.
And you shall restore the face of the earth.
Amen.

Blessings Before and After Meals

*B*lessed be you, Lord God of the universe,
who brings forth bread from the earth
and makes glad the heart of all
    who praise you.
                  (Ancient Hebrew prayer)

*C*ome, Lord Jesus, be our guest
and bless what you have given us.
                  (German family grace)

*J*esus, God-with-us, you not only enjoyed
a meal with your friends,
but you even prepared a jolly good breakfast
for your weary Apostles, broiling fresh fish
    just for them.
Be with us now as we partake of food
    and friendship.
For these gifts and your many other blessings,
we thank you, generous, hospitable One.

We thank you, God, not only for
this food
we have shared but also for the joy
of friendship,
which has turned this meal into a true agape.

Prayer Before a Crucifix

*L*ook down on me, good and gentle Jesus,
while before your face I humbly kneel,
and pray and beseech you
to fix deep in my heart
lively sentiments of faith, hope, and charity,
true contrition for my sins, and a firm
purpose of amendment.
While I contemplate with great love
and tender pity your five most precious
wounds,
pondering over them and calling to mind
the word
which David, your prophet, said of you,
my Jesus:
"They have pierced my hands and my feet;
they have numbered all my bones."

(Thomas Aquinas)

Breastplate of Saint Patrick

I rise up today,
   the power of God directing me,
the strength of God supporting me,
the wisdom of God guiding me,
the eye of God looking before me,
the ear of God listening to me,
the hand of God protecting me,
the way of God stretching before me,
the shield of God defending me,
the angels of God guarding me,
   against snares of devils,
   against temptations,
   against vices of any kind.
Christ be with me, Christ before me,
      Christ behind me,
Christ in me, Christ beneath me,
      Christ above me,
Christ on my right hand,
      Christ on my left hand,
Christ where I sit, Christ where I rise,
Christ in the mouth of everyone who
      speaks of me,
Christ in the heart of everyone who
      thinks of me,
Christ in every eye that sees me,
Christ in every ear that hears me.

An Irish Prayer

*D*ear Lord,
  be thou a bright flame before me;
be thou a guiding star above me;
be thou a smooth path below me;
be thou a kindly shepherd ahead of me,
today, tonight, forever.

(Columba of Iona)

An Irish Blessing

With the first light of sun,
  God bless you.
When the day is done,
God bless you.
In your smiles and your tears,
God bless you.
Through each day of your years,
God bless you.

An Early Gaelic Blessing
when Parting

*M*ay the grace of Christ uphold you
and the Father's love enfold you.
May the Holy Spirit guide you
and all joy and peace be with you
now and to eternity.

A slight revision of this prayer can be an
encouraging blessing as a patient leaves for
surgery or other complicated procedures.

*M*ay the grace of Christ uphold you,
and the Father's love enfold you.
May the Holy Spirit strengthen you
and guide all those who will be caring for you
in these next hours. Our prayers follow you;
may you feel Christ's healing power and love.
Amen.

Prayer of Saint Richard of Chichester

*T*hank you, Lord Jesus Christ,
  for all the benefits and blessings
you have given me,
for all the pains you have borne for me.
Merciful friend, brother, and redeemer,
may I know you more clearly,
love you more dearly,
and follow you more nearly,
day by day.

Amazing Grace

*A*mazing grace! How sweet the sound
that saved a wretch like me.
I once was lost, but now am found,
was blind, but now I see!
'Twas grace that taught my heart to fear,
and grace my fears relieved.
How precious did that grace appear,
the hour I first believed!
The Lord has promised good to me;
his word my hope secures.
He will my shield and portion be
as long as life endures.
Through many dangers, toils, and snares,
I have already come.
'Tis grace has brought me safe thus far,
and grace will lead me home.
When we've been there ten thousand years,
bright shining as the sun,
we've no less days to sing God's praise
than when we'd first begun.

(John Newton)

O God, Our Help in Ages Past

O God, our help in ages past, our hope in
    years to come,
our shelter from the stormy blast, and our
    eternal home.
Beneath the shadow of your throne
    your saints have dwelt secure;
sufficient in your arm alone, and our defense
    is sure.
Before the hills in order stood, or earth
    received her frame,
from everlasting you are God, to endless years
    the same.
A thousand ages in your sight are like
    an evening gone,
short as the watch that ends the night before
    the rising sun.
Time, like an ever-rolling stream, bears all
    our lives away;
they fly, forgotten, as a dream dies
    at the op'ning day.
O God, our help in ages past, our hope
    for years to come,
be now our guide while life shall last, and our
    eternal home.
    (Isaac Watts, based on Psalm 90:1–6,12)

Lead, Kindly Light

*L*ead, Kindly Light, amid the encircling
  gloom,
   lead thou me on!
The night is dark, and I am far from home—
   lead thou me on!
Keep thou my feet; I do not ask to see
the distant scene,—one step enough for me.

I was not ever thus, nor pray'd that thou
   shouldst lead me on.
I loved to choose and see my path, but now
   lead thou me on!
I loved the garish day, and, spite of fears,
pride ruled my will: remember not past years.

So long thy power hath blest me, sure it still
   will lead me on;
O'er moor and fen, o'er crag and torrent, till
   the night is gone;
and with the morn those angel faces smile
which I have loved long since, and lost awhile.

(John Henry Cardinal Newman)

A Prayer for All God's Own

We beg you, Lord, to help and
defend us.
Deliver the oppressed, pity the lowly,
raise the fallen, show yourself
to the needy, and heal the sick.
Bring back those who have gone astray,
feed the hungry, lift up the weak,
take off the prisoner's chains.
Make every nation come to know
that you alone are God,
that Jesus Christ is your Son,
and that we are your people,
the sheep that you pasture.
Give concord and peace to us
and to all living on the earth,
as you gave them to our fathers
when they prayed to you, believing firmly,
ready to obey the All Powerful, the All Holy.
You alone have the power to do this for us,
this and more than this.
We thank you for all this through Him,
now at this moment, in every generation,
age after age. Amen.

(Clement of Rome)

A Christopher Song

*L*et's sing a song to God.
  A song of thanks
    for understanding, love, and life.
A song of thanks
    for children and for those
        who've grown older,
    for those whose wisdom has guided us,
    for those who taught us to love.
Let's sing a song of praise to God
    for all that God has made.
By living and sharing God's gifts—
    we sing our songs to God.

I Believe

I believe in the sun,
   even when it is not shining.
I believe in love,
even when I feel it not.
I believe in God,
even when He is silent.

> (Words written on a cellar wall in
> Cologne, Germany, after World War II)

Let Nothing Disturb You

*L*et nothing disturb you.
Let nothing make you afraid.
All things are passing;
God alone never changes.
Patience gains all things.
If you have God,
you will want for nothing.
God alone suffices.

(Teresa of Ávila)

The Serenity Prayer

*D*ear God,
give us the grace
to accept with serenity
the things we cannot change,
courage to change the things we must,
and the wisdom to know the difference.

(Reinhold Niebuhr)

God, Teach Me

God,
teach me
to face the discomfort
of knowing myself
and to give others
the benefit of the doubt.
Make me tireless
in seeking to do your will,
which in my heart
I recognize
more than I care to admit.
Weakness, slowness,
and mistakes are part
of the human scene.
Make me honest enough
to treat the inadequacies
of other people
the way I would want them
—and you—
to deal with mine. Amen.

(A Christopher prayer)

The Lord's Promise

*L*isten!
I am standing at the door,
knocking;
if you hear my voice
and open the door,
I will come in to you
and eat with you,
and you with me.

(Revelation 3:20)

God Alone

*G*od, of your goodness,
give me yourself,
for you are enough for me, and
I can ask for nothing . . . less
which can pay you full worship.
And if I ask for anything . . . less
always I am in want;
but only in you do I have everything.

(Julian of Norwich)

The Love of God

God, with your servant Paul, I confess:
"I am convinced
that neither death,
nor life,
nor angels,
nor rulers,
nor things present,
nor things to come,
nor powers,
nor height,
nor depth,
nor anything else in all creation,
will be able to separate us
from the love of God
in Christ Jesus." Amen. Alleluia!

(Romans 8:38–39)

Evening Prayers

Abide with Us, Lord

*A*bide with us, Lord,
for it is toward evening
and the day is far spent;
abide with us and with your whole church.
Abide with us in the evening of the day,
in the evening of life,
in the evening of the world.
Abide with us and with all your faithful ones,
O Lord, in time and eternity.

(Lutheran Manual of Prayer)

Twilight Thoughts

Grant, O generous Creator,
that we may live in your love,
die in your favor,
rest in your peace,
arise in your power,
reign in your glory,
for the sake of your Son,
Jesus Christ, our redeemer.

(William Laud)

An Evening Hymn

*I*nspiring light,
  O holy glory,
of the undying, heavenly Father,
the holy, blessed Jesus Christ,
the sun has set, and now,
seeing the lamp that lights the evening,
we praise the Father and the Son
and God the Holy Spirit.
Prayer is due you at all times
from grateful hearts.
O Son of God, O Giver of life,
therefore does the world give you glory.

(An early Christian prayer)

As the Shadows Fall

*T*he shadows fall, but end of day
fills the eye with brightness;
the infinite heavens glow,
and all creation sings its hymn of glory.
With hope, therefore, we pray for light
within:
O God, reveal yourself; hide no more;
let your face shine on all who seek you.

Eternal and infinite God, banish
our darkness!
Be present to us as the sudden light
that lifts the heart and brings us joy.

Then shall we be at peace,
O God, whose peaceful shelter we seek
through all the days and nights of our lives.

(Gates of Prayer)

Thank You, O God

*T*hank you, O God,
   for your care and protection this day,
keeping me safe from physical and spiritual
     harm.
I now place the work of this day in your
     hands,
trusting that you will redeem my errors
and turn my achievements to your glory.
And now I ask you to work within me,
trusting that you will use the hours of rest
to create in me a new heart and a new soul.
Let my mind, which through the day
has been directed to my work,
through the evening be wholly directed
     at you.
Let me rest tonight in your arms,
     and let me awake
tomorrow, strong, eager to serve you
     faithfully.

(Jacob Boehme)

Prayer at Eventide

O Lord,
whatever sins I have committed this day
in word, deed, or thought,
forgive me, for you are gracious
    and compassionate,
and you love all those whom you have made.
Grant me a peaceful, undisturbed sleep;
command my guardian angel to watch
    over me.
Protect this night all who labor for our good;
give them strength and reward them
    for their dedication.
Bless, please, my family, friends, and relatives.
Keep them in your love,
so that we may all continue to praise you,
Father, Son, and Holy Spirit,
now and forever. Amen.

(A Russian Orthodox prayer)

Shelter Us, Father

*C*ause us, our Father,
to lie down in peace,
and to rise again to enjoy life.
Spread over us the covering of your peace,
guide us with your good counsel,
and save us for the sake of your name.
Be a shield about us, turning away
every enemy, disease, violence, hunger,
and sorrow.
Shelter us in the shadow of your wings,
for you are a God who guards
and protects us,
a ruler of mercy and compassion.
Guard us when we go out and when we
come in,
to enjoy life and peace both now and forever,
and spread over us the shelter of your peace.
Blessed are you, O Lord,
who spreads the shelter of peace over us,
over your people Israel,
and over all the world.

(Gates of Prayer)

We Confess, Lord

*W*e confess that in our lives we do not
always choose the way of peace.
We spread gossip which fans the flames
of hatred.
We are ready to make any sacrifices when
Caesar demands—
but few when God invites.
We worship the false god of security. . . .
We hold out one hand in friendship—
but keep a weapon in the other behind
our back.
We have divided your body of people
into those
we trust and those we do not.
Huge problems challenge us in the world—
but our greed, fear, and selfishness prevent us
from uniting to solve them.
Lord,
we need your help and forgiveness,
your reconciling power.

(Pax Christi)

Into Your Loving Hands

*I*nto your loving hands,
Creator God,
we place ourselves
and all those who are dear to us,
especially those who minister here,
taking care of our many needs.
May the gift of your presence,
maternal, nourishing, loving,
support us all the day long.
Grant that we never lose sight of you,
but help us to praise and glorify you
by extending love and concern to all
whom we encounter,
so that now as night comes,
we may again thank you and ask
     your blessing
of peace of heart, bodily rest, and safety
until tomorrow dawns.

A Night Prayer
for Freedom from Anxiety

*D*o not fear what may happen tomorrow.
The same loving Father who cares for
you today,
will care for you tomorrow and every day.
Either he will shield you from suffering,
or he will give you unfailing strength
to bear it.
Be at peace then, and put aside all anxious
thoughts
and fearful imaginings. Trust in the Giver
of all good gifts.

(Francis de Sales)

*W*hatever is true, whatever is honorable,
whatever is just, whatever is pure,
whatever is pleasing, whatever is commend-
able, if there is any excellence and if there is
anything worthy of praise, think about these
things . . . and the God of peace will be
with you.

(Philippians 4:8–9)

Prayer Before Sleep

Blessed are you, O Lord our God,
King of the universe,
who makes the bands of sleep to fall upon
    my eyes,
and slumber upon my eyelids.
May it be your will, O Lord
my God and the God of my fathers,
to suffer me to lie down in peace
and to let me rise up again in peace.
Let not my thoughts trouble me,
nor evil dreams nor fancies,
but let my rest be perfect before you. . . .
Blessed are you, O Lord,
who gives light to the whole world
    by your glory.

(Hebrew Prayer Book)

A Friendship Prayer

L ord God, well-spring of all love,
fathomless sea of kindness and grace,
make us co-heirs of your peace.
Kindle in us bright flames of your love,
strengthen us in the confession of your
truths,
bless our efforts to live these truths.
Unite us to yourself
and to one another
in firm, unbreakable bonds of peace,
that we, one in heart and soul upon this
earth,
may be one in the eternal feast of your
presence.
There we shall glorify you,
Father—Son—Spirit,
in your everlasting dwelling place. Amen.
(An ancient Gaelic prayer)

Prayer for My Friends

O Lord Jesus,
  give my friends
hearts to love you always.
Bless each with
a will to choose you,
a memory to recall you,
a mind to think of you,
a soul always united to you.
And may you, the God of compassion
    and mercy,
love and protect them, now and forever.
    Amen.

(Augustine)

Prayer for Absent Friends

*H*oly, living God,
   bless my friends who no longer come
      to visit me.
I am not blaming them,
for I know exactly what keeps them away.
There was a time, not so long ago,
when I, too, was reluctant to visit
      the suffering.
I was fearful that I might betray my distress,
say the wrong thing, or worse—
murmur meaningless banalities, so trite
      and irksome
to those in pain of any kind.
I understand my friends' reluctance to come;
after all, what can they do or say?
Nevertheless, I would love to see them—
just a pop-in visit,
      or a "How are you doing?" call;
even an e-mail message would be
      heartwarming.
Yet I understand, and you, Christ,
      most certainly do,
because your friends stayed away
      at crucial times, too.

Just as you welcomed back and forgave
    your truants,
may I continue to love and pray for my
    absent friends.
Bless them, my God; inspirit them
    with compassionate love.

Lord, We Turn to You

*L*ord, you give meaning to our hopes,
to our struggles and our strivings.
Without you we are lost, our lives empty.
And so when all else fails us, we turn to you!
In the stillness of the night,
when the outer darkness enters the soul;
in the press of the crowd, when we walk alone
though yearning for companionship;
and when in agony we are bystanders
        to our own confusion,
we look to you for hope and peace.

Lord, we do not ask for a life of ease,
for happiness without alloy.
Instead we ask you to teach us to be
        uncomplaining and unafraid.
In our darkness help us to find your light.
Give us strength to face life with hope
        and courage,
that even from its discords and conflicts
we may draw blessing.
Make us understand that life calls us
not merely to enjoy the richness of the earth,
but to exult in heights attained after the toil
        of climbing.

Let our darkness be dispelled by your love,
that we may rise above fear and failure,
   our steps sustained by faith.

(Gates of Prayer)

You Are Our Peace

O God,
you are peace.
From you is peace and to you is peace.
Let us live, O Lord,
in peace and receive us in your paradise,
the abode of peace.
Yours is the majesty and the praise,
we hear and we obey.
Grant us your forgiveness, Lord,
and to you be our becoming.

(The Prophet Mohammed)

Grant Us Peace

Grant us peace, your most precious gift,
Eternal Source of peace,
and give us the will to proclaim its message
to all the peoples of the earth.
Bless our country, that it may always be
a stronghold of peace, and its advocate
    among the nations.
May contentment reign within its borders,
health and happiness within its homes.
Strengthen the bonds of friendship
    among the inhabitants
of all lands. And may the love of your name
hallow every home and every heart.
Blessed is the eternal God, the source
    of peace.

(Gates of Prayer)

Lord, Help Me to Rest

*L*ord, help me to rest in peace tonight,
so that I may rise, refreshed and ready
to spend a new and blessed day in your
  service.
And if that means hours in bed, therapy,
or whatever is scheduled for the next day,
let me accept it with grace and courage—and
gratitude for all that is being done for me.
The winter of my heart is gradually
  being replaced
by springtime, for I'm recovering! *Deo gratias!*

I Will Lay Me Down

I will lay me down in peace
  and take my rest:
for it is you, Lord, only,
that makes me dwell in safety.
Into your hands, O Lord,
I commend my spirit,
for you have redeemed me,
O Lord, God of truth.

(Compline)

Until the Shadows Lengthen

O Lord,
support us all the day long,
until the shadows lengthen
and the evening comes,
and the busy world is hushed,
and the fever of life is over,
and our work is done.
Then, Lord, in [your] mercy,
grant us a safe lodging,
and a holy rest,
and peace at the last;
through Jesus Christ our Lord.

(John Henry Cardinal Newman)

Into Your Hands, O Lord

Into your hands, O Lord and Father,
we commend this night our souls
    and our bodies,
our parents, our children, and our homes,
our relatives, friends, and neighbors,
those who govern and guide us,
all who need your pity and protection,
and those who have gone to their eternal rest.
Enlighten us, the living, with your holy grace,
and help us so that we may never
    be separated from you,
the one God, Father, Son, and Holy Spirit.

(Edmund of Abingdon)

Save Us, O Lord

Save us, O Lord, while waking,
and guard us while sleeping,
that when we wake, we may watch
    with Christ,
and when we sleep, we may rest in peace.

(Roman Breviary)

Be Present, O Merciful God

*B*e present, O merciful God,
and protect us through the silent hours
of the night, that we who are wearied
by the changes and chances of this
fleeting world
may repose upon [your] eternal
changelessness,
through the everlasting Christ our Lord.
(Gelasian Sacramentary)

Acknowledgments *(continued)*

The psalms in this book are from *Psalms Anew: In Inclusive Language,* compiled by Nancy Schreck and Maureen Leach (Winona, MN: Saint Mary's Press, 1986). Copyright © 1986 by Saint Mary's Press. All rights reserved.

The scriptural quotations on pages 30, 62, and 72 are freely adapted and are not to be interpreted or used as official translations of the Bible.

All other scriptural quotations in this book are from the New Revised Standard Version of the Bible. Copyright © 1989 by the Division of Christian Education of the National Council of the Churches of Christ in the United States of America. All rights reserved.

The excerpt by Thomas Merton on page 10 is from *The Living Bread,* by Thomas Merton (New York: Dell Publishing Company, 1959), page 134. Copyright © 1956 by the Abbey of Our Lady of Gethsemani.

The excerpt by Michael Downey on page 10 is from *Clothed in Christ,* by Michael Downey (New York: Crossroad, 1987), page 126.

The excerpt by Victor Frankl on page 15, the Sanskrit poem on page 24, the adaptation of a Christopher song on page 125, and the Christopher prayer on page 129 are from *Christopher News Notes,* nos. 392, 357, 357, and 392, respectively. Used with permission.

The excerpts by Jacob Boehme on page 25, by Augustine on page 42, and by Jacob Boehme (adapted) on page 139 are from *The HarperCollins Book of Prayers: A Treasury of Prayers Through the Ages,* compiled by Robert Van de Weyer (San Francisco: HarperSanFrancisco, 1993), pages 67, 44, and 68, respectively. Copyright © 1993 by Robert Van de Weyer.